Railroad Accident Report

Rear-End Collision of National Railroad Passenger Corporation (Amtrak) Train P286 with CSXT Freight Train Q620 on the CSX Railroad at Syracuse, New York
February 5, 2001

NTSB/RAR-01/04

PB2001-916304

Notation 7411

Adopted November 27, 2001

National Transportation Safety Board
490 L'Enfant Plaza, S.W.
Washington, D.C. 20594

National Transportation Safety Board. 2001. *Rear-End Collision of National Railroad Passenger Corporation (Amtrak) Train P286 With CSXT Freight Train Q620 on the CSX Railroad at Syracuse, New York.* **Railroad Accident Report NTSB/RAR-01/04. Washington, DC.**

Abstract: At about 11:40 a.m., eastern standard time, on February 5, 2001, eastbound Amtrak train 286, with 100 passengers and 4 crewmembers, struck the rear of eastbound CSX Transportation (CSXT) freight train Q620 on the CSXT Railroad near Syracuse, New York. On impact, the lead Amtrak locomotive unit and four of the train's five cars derailed. The rear truck of the last car of the 92-car CSXT freight train derailed, and the car lost a portion of its load of lumber. At the time of impact, the passenger train was traveling 35 mph; the freight train was traveling 7 mph. The accident resulted in injuries to all 4 crewmembers and 58 of the passengers aboard the Amtrak train. No CSXT crewmember was injured. A small amount of diesel fuel spilled from the fuel tank on the lead Amtrak locomotive unit, but no fire resulted. Total damages were estimated to be about $280,600.

The safety issues addressed in the report are the lack of a positive train control system to prevent train collisions, the adequacy of Amtrak's procedures for ensuring that appliances on Amtrak trains are always properly secured, and the adequacy of maps used by emergency response personnel for railroad accidents.

As a result of this accident investigation, the Safety Board made recommendations to the Federal Railroad Administration, the National Emergency Number Association, the Association of American Railroads, the American Short Line and Regional Railroad Association, and the National Railroad Passenger Corporation.

Contents

Executive Summary

At about 11:40 a.m., eastern standard time, on February 5, 2001, eastbound Amtrak train 286, with 100 passengers and 4 crewmembers, struck the rear of eastbound CSX Transportation (CSXT) freight train Q620 on the CSXT Railroad near Syracuse, New York. On impact, the lead Amtrak locomotive unit and four of the train's five cars derailed. The rear truck of the last car of the 92-car CSXT freight train derailed, and the car lost a portion of its load of lumber. At the time of impact, the passenger train was traveling 35 mph; the freight train was traveling 7 mph. The accident resulted in injuries to all 4 crewmembers and 58 of the passengers aboard the Amtrak train. No CSXT crewmember was injured. A small amount of diesel fuel spilled from the fuel tank on the lead Amtrak locomotive unit, but no fire resulted. Total damages were estimated to be about $280,600.

The National Transportation Safety Board determines that the probable cause of the February 5, 2001, collision of Amtrak train 286 with the rear of CSXT freight train Q620 was the Amtrak engineer's inattention to the operation of his train, which led to his failure to recognize and comply with the speed limit imposed by the governing wayside signal, and the lack of any safety redundancy system capable of preventing a collision in the event of human failure.

The safety issues addressed in the report are as follows:

- The lack of a positive train control system to prevent train collisions;

- The adequacy of Amtrak's procedures for ensuring that appliances on Amtrak trains are always properly secured;

- The adequacy of maps used by emergency response personnel for railroad accidents.

As a result of its investigation of this accident, the National Transportation Safety Board makes safety recommendations to the Federal Railroad Administration, the National Emergency Number Association, the American Short Line and Regional Railroad Association, and the National Railroad Passenger Corporation (Amtrak).

Factual Information

Accident Synopsis

At about 11:40 a.m., eastern standard time, on February 5, 2001, eastbound Amtrak train 286, with 100 passengers and 4 crewmembers, struck the rear of eastbound CSX Transportation (CSXT) freight train Q620 on the CSXT Railroad near Syracuse, New York. On impact, the lead Amtrak locomotive unit and four of the train's five cars derailed. The rear truck of the last car of the 92-car CSXT freight train derailed, and the car lost a portion of its load of lumber. At the time of impact, the passenger train was traveling 35 mph; the freight train was traveling 7 mph. The accident resulted in injuries to all 4 crewmembers and 58 of the passengers aboard the Amtrak train. No CSXT crewmember was injured. A small amount of diesel fuel spilled from the fuel tank on the lead Amtrak locomotive unit, but no fire resulted. Total damages were estimated to be about $280,600.

Accident Narrative

Eastbound Amtrak train 286, en route from Niagara Falls, New York, to New York City, arrived at Syracuse Station at about 11:23 a.m. on Monday, February 5, 2001. The train consisted of two locomotive units followed by a café car and four coaches. Of the four Amtrak crewmembers aboard, only the engineer was in the locomotive cab. During the stop at Syracuse, the inbound engineer, who operated the train into Syracuse, was to be relieved by another engineer (the accident engineer) for the next 2 1/2-hour leg of the journey, which would take the train to Albany, New York. (See figure 1.)

Figure 1. Route of Amtrak train 286 from Niagara Falls to New York City.

The accident engineer normally operated trains between Syracuse and his home terminal at Rensselaer (Albany). On this day, however, the accident engineer had boarded train 286 at Depew, New York, and had traveled to Syracuse in the café car. About 10 minutes before arriving in Syracuse on train 286, and as required by Amtrak rules,[1] the conductor briefed the accident engineer in preparation for that day's assignment. The conductor also briefed the accident engineer on three current bulletins[2] and told him about a contingent of disabled people on board bound for Albany. The engineer stated that before the train reached Syracuse, he attempted to call the dispatcher on his cell phone to "register," or notify the train dispatcher that he would be the outbound engineer. He said he could not reach the dispatcher by phone, so he decided to wait and radio the dispatcher from the locomotive.

At the Syracuse station, the inbound and outbound engineers got off the train and met on the station platform. According to the accident engineer, the inbound engineer said that he had a *medium approach* signal[3] coming into Syracuse station. Also, according to the accident engineer, the inbound engineer said that the train had operated normally except that, because of the extra weight of two locomotive units,[4] a little more braking time was required and the brakes were therefore "sluggish."

After the briefing, the inbound engineer left and the accident engineer mounted the control cab of the lead locomotive unit. With the engineer as the only crewmember in the cab, the train departed the Syracuse station at about 11:33 a.m., 20 minutes behind schedule. The train dispatcher had lined Amtrak train 286 from No. 7 track (on which the train had entered the station), through the interlocking at CP (control point) 290 (about 3/4 mile from the station), onto main track No. 1, the northernmost of two parallel east-west main line tracks. Because of repairs being performed on main track No. 2, that track was temporarily out of service, and the dispatcher was using No. 1 track for all through trains, as well as for trains bound for DeWitt yard. When Amtrak train 286 entered track No. 1, it would be following CSXT freight train Q620. (See figure 2.)

---

[1] Northeast Operating Rules Committee (NORAC) rules, 7th edition, effective January 17, 2000.

[2] Bulletins are temporary official notices that affect the movement, safety, or operation of a train, such as slow sections of track and other temporary hazards.

[3] Under NORAC rules, a *medium approach* signal aspect is a red light over a flashing yellow light that requires the engineer to slow the train to 30 mph and be prepared to stop at the next signal.

[4] The train on February 5 had two locomotives, although it was normally operated with a single unit.

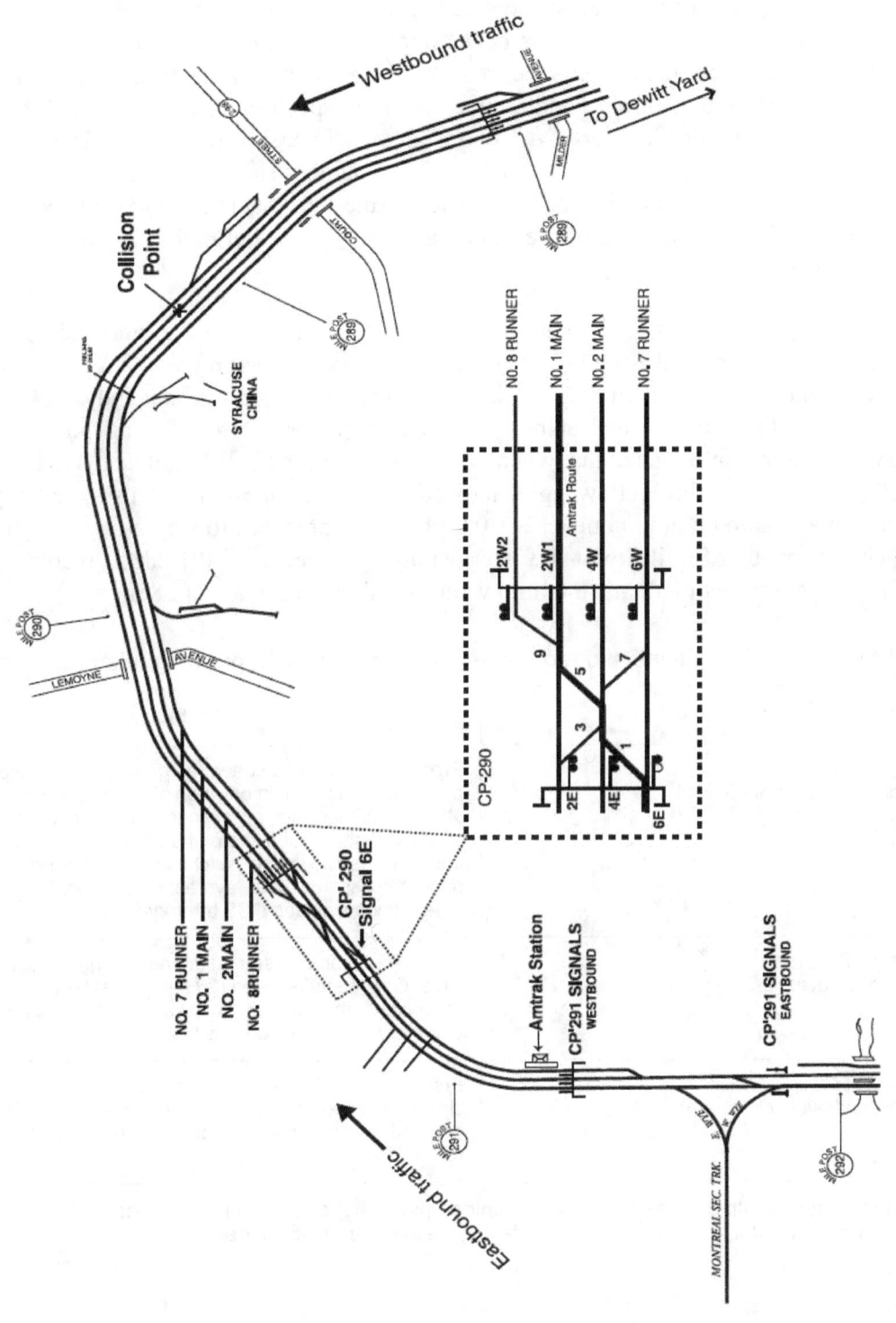

Figure 2. Accident area (not to scale).

According to the engineer, his first task upon departure was to make a running brake test, as required by Amtrak rules, in order to determine the effectiveness of the air brake system. As soon as he had accelerated the train to 30 mph (about 1/4 mile from the station while still on track No. 7), he began applying the brakes. According to the lead locomotive event recorder, the engineer reduced the brake pipe (air) pressure from 105 to 93 psi, which applied the brakes and reduced the train speed by 5 mph. Satisfied that the brakes were functioning properly, the engineer then released the brakes. The running brake test took about 19 seconds to perform. The engineer stated that he had the brakes applied when he saw signal 6E at the entrance to the interlocking at CP 290. When the brakes were released, the head of the train was about 1,700 feet before signal 6E, at the entrance to CP 290.

According to the signal computer memory log, signal 6E at the time Amtrak train 286 approached displayed a "solid," or steady, red light over a solid yellow light. The solid red-over-yellow aspect of this signal display is called *restricting*, and indicates to the engineer that he is to proceed at restricted speed. (See table 1.) During postaccident interviews, the engineer stated that when he saw signal 6E, he believed it displayed a solid red light over a flashing yellow light, indicating *medium approach*. This signal aspect would have required him to not exceed 30 mph and be prepared to stop at the next signal (which was about 2.7 miles past the interlocking, at milepost [MP] 288). According to locomotive event recorder data, the train went past signal 6E at about 28 mph.

Table 1. Signal indications and requirements under NORAC operating rules.[a]

Signal Indication	Requirements
Restricting (solid red over solid yellow)	Proceed at restricting speed (no greater than 15 mph, prepared to stop within one-half of the sight distance, short of another train, misaligned switch, broken rail, or other obstacle) until the entire train has cleared all interlockings and spring switches and the lead wheels have (1) passed a more favorable fixed signal, or (2) entered non-signaled DCS territory.
Medium Approach (solid red over flashing yellow)	Proceed prepared to stop at the next signal. Trains exceeding medium speed (30 mph) must begin reduction to medium speed as soon as the *medium approach* signal is clearly visible.
Medium Clear (solid red over solid green)	Proceed at medium speed (30 mph) until the train clears all interlockings or spring switches, then proceed at normal speed (maximum authorized speed [in this accident, 60 mph]).

[a] Northeast Operating Rules Advisory Committee (NORAC) operating rules govern movements of all trains, including Amtrak, that operate on this section of CSXT track.

The engineer later said that he had never gotten a restricting signal at 6E. He said that he got a *medium approach* aspect at signal 6E "40 percent of the time," and that "the majority of the time," the signal would show a *"clear"* aspect. What the engineer referred to as a *clear* signal was actually *medium clear*, which was the most permissive signal possible at signal 6E. Under a *medium clear* indication, the engineer is to slow to medium speed (30 mph) until the train clears the interlocking, after which he may accelerate to the maximum authorized speed of 60 mph. Although the speed is limited to 30 mph, the *medium clear* signal implies that no train occupies the block ahead.

At the time the train passed the signal, the isolation switch (on the back wall of the locomotive cab) of the lead locomotive was in the "Isolate" position, meaning that although the lead locomotive's diesel engines were running, the traction motors were not powering the wheels; all the motive power was being provided by the trailing locomotive. According to the locomotive event recorder, about 1/4 mile into the interlocking, the engineer turned the isolation switch to the "Run" position,[5] after which the traction motors of both locomotives were powering the train. At the time this occurred, the throttle was in the eighth notch, the highest power position. With the tractive effort thus doubled, the train began to increase its speed. The engineer later said he did not recall turning the isolation switch.

Over the next minute, the train speed increased from 29 to 59 mph. As the train accelerated, the engineer said that he was retrieving track bulletins from his bag. He said:

> I had the bag down to the…left of me…and I was kneeling down…trying to find a bulletin. My eyes were down toward the floor. It seemed like just a minute–30 seconds…. And when I looked up, I was already coming around the curve. I didn't realize the speed had picked up.

He said:

> When you're the only man in the cab, there's a number of things you have to tend to, such as looking at a bulletin, getting a drink of water, whatever. If you were to stop for every time your eyes are distracted mainly to the front, you would never arrive anywhere.

Meanwhile, CSXT train Q620, just ahead of the Amtrak train on track No. 1, had received a *stop-and-proceed* signal indication at the signal at MP 288. The Amtrak engineer said,

> I looked up–there was the rear end of the train [Q620]. At first, I thought [that train is] on track 8 because…my last [signal] indication wouldn't give me that. As I rounded the bend a little more, [the end of the freight train] came into more focus, and at that time [the Amtrak train] just wouldn't stop, I was in emergency, and I I ran into the rear end.

---

[5] Because of the location of the isolation switch, the engineer had to leave his seat to set or reposition the switch.

According to locomotive event recorder data, Amtrak train 286 went into emergency braking at about 57 mph about 840 feet from the rear of train Q620. At impact, the Amtrak train was traveling 35 mph. The freight train, which had proceeded again after stopping, was then moving eastbound at 7 mph, resulting in an effective impact speed of about 28 mph. The accident occurred about 11:40 a.m. (See figures 3 and 4.)

Figure 3. Looking east shortly after the collision, with the Syracuse China plant and parking lot on the right.

Figure 4. Postaccident positions of the end of the CSXT freight train and the lead Amtrak locomotive unit.

Emergency Response

Crewmembers from CSXT train Q620 and Amtrak train 286 immediately notified the CSXT train dispatcher after the collision. The dispatcher asked for the location of the head end of the Amtrak train and was told by an Amtrak train 286 conductor that the train was east of CP 290 and he "could see milepost 290."

About 11:43 a.m., the CSXT dispatching center at Selkirk, New York, notified the Onondaga County Department of Emergency Communications 911 telephone operator of a train accident with multiple minor injuries, but no fire. The CSXT dispatcher provided a milepost (MP 290) and street name (Factory Avenue) to assist responders in locating the accident; however, mileposts were not included on maps used by the Onondaga Emergency Communications Center (ECC). The ECC provided responding units with the locations of Lemoyne Avenue or Factory Avenue, which are about a mile from the accident.

At 11:45 a.m., a passenger aboard the Amtrak train called 911 by cell phone and said that the train had left Syracuse about 10 minutes before, heading east toward Albany. The caller said that there were injured passengers aboard and that there was "smoke" in his compartment, but no fire.

At 11:45 a.m., the East Syracuse Fire Department was dispatched to the accident site, followed by the Mattydale Fire Department and the Lyncourt Fire Department. At 11:55 a.m., the chief of the Lyncourt Fire Department assumed incident command and established a command post in the parking lot behind Syracuse China Company.

At 12:04 p.m., Rural/Metro Medical Services units responded to the scene. At 12:06 p.m., the incident commander declared a Level 3 MCI (multiple casualty incident).[6] At 12:12 p.m., the first medical service unit arrived on scene, and a transportation triage area was established in the rear of a nearby business parking lot. At 12:22 p.m., the Rural/Metro trailer arrived at the parking lot. Patients were evaluated, treated, and transported to local hospitals. The first patient left the scene at about 1:04 p.m. According to the incident commander, 44 passengers were transported to the hospital. The firefighters assisted in the evacuation of the passengers. The last patient left the scene at approximately 1:44 p.m. The majority of the fire units were then released.

At 11:45 a.m., the Onondaga County Sheriff's Office was dispatched to the scene of the accident. Police units from DeWitt, Syracuse, and the New York State Police Department responded to the site. Officers assisted with traffic control, security of the scene, and the protection of personal property. About 21 members of the Onondaga County Sheriff's Office took part in the response and investigation.

Amtrak representatives received notification that something had happened east of the Syracuse Amtrak station at 11:40 a.m. Local ticket agents from the Syracuse Amtrak Station responded immediately to assist at the scene. Amtrak's Empire Service response

---

[6] Onondoga County defines an MCI level 3 as more than 10 patients.

team was assembled in the Empire Service Command Center in Albany at noon; the team departed for Syracuse at 12:20 p.m. Members of the Empire Service response team began arriving on scene at 2 p.m.

CSXT representatives received a call at 11:43 a.m. reporting the collision. At 11:58 a.m., the DeWitt terminal superintendent arrived at the scene from the north side. At 12:05 p.m., additional CSXT personnel arrived on scene to offer their assistance. The superintendent arrived at the command center at 1:15 p.m. to aid in the response and investigation.

As required by 49 *Code of Federal Regulations* (CFR) 239.105, Amtrak held a debriefing and critique with all the accident emergency response organizations on April 12, 2001, in Syracuse. At this meeting, a representative from the Onondaga County 911 Communications Control Center said that the center now includes mileposts locations on its maps.

Injuries

The injuries ranged from contusions and lacerations to fractures. Most passengers were treated and released the same day from area hospitals. (See table 2.)

Table 2. Injuries

Injury Scale[a]	CSX Operating Crew	Amtrak Operating Crew	Amtrak On-Board Service Crew	Amtrak Passengers	Total
Fatal	0	0	0	0	0
Serious	0	0	0	4	4
Minor	0	3	1	54	58
None	2	0	0	42	44
Total	2	3	1	100	106

[a]49 *Code of Federal Regulations* 830.2 defines fatal injury as "any injury which results in death within 30 days of the accident" and serious injury as "an injury which: (1) requires hospitalization for more than 48 hours, commencing within 7 days from the date the injury was received; (2) results in a fracture of any bone (except simple fractures of fingers, toes, or nose); (3) causes severe hemorrhages, nerve, or tendon damage; (4) involves any internal organ; or (5) involves second or third-degree burns, or any burn affecting more than 5 percent of the body surface."

Damage

General

Upon impact, the CSXT freight train end-of-train device was destroyed. The brake pipe on the last car was also severed, which caused the CSXT train brakes to apply in emergency. The rear truck of the last freight car derailed. The last freight car lost a portion of its load of lumber. (See figure 5.) Total CSXT damage was $7,581 for cars and lading. Except for a section of track that had rolled onto its side under the derailed rear freight car, the track structure remained relatively undisturbed with no significant change in track structure or geometry. Cost of repositioning and re-spiking the rolled rail was estimated at about $600.

Figure 5. Damaged rear freight car of CSXT freight train Q620.

The Amtrak lead locomotive, Amtrak 414 (figure 6), suffered damage to the nose, pilot, plow, front coupler, draft gear, coupler pocket, front collision post at deck level, electrical wiring and associated conduits, front trucks and derailed right and left No. 2 wheels, and No. 1 traction motor. Total damage was estimated to be $200,000.

Figure 6. Damaged lead locomotive of Amtrak train 286.

The trailing locomotive, Amtrak 411, remained on the rails and suffered no damage. Damage to the café car and three coaches totaled $80,000.

Appliance Retention

On February 7, 2001, Safety Board investigators examined Amtrak café car 48910 at DeWitt Yard. They found one convection oven displaced from its normal locked position. The oven was on the counter between the wall and the coffee maker. The hinged retaining bar, which folds down over the top of the oven to secure it in place, was unlocked. No injuries were attributed to unsecured appliances.

According to Amtrak officials, appliance securement checks are performed during scheduled maintenance, which for passenger cars is every 120 days and for food service cars, such as the café car involved in the accident, is every 60 days. Café car 48910 had had its most recent 60-day maintenance on December 12, 2000.

Daily or initial terminal inspections do not include a securement check of appliances. During turnaround equipment servicing, written reports of mechanical defects are noted, and repairs are made before departure. According to Amtrak, the turnaround inspection for onboard appliances is a cursory inspection with no formal list or book of required tasks.

Passenger car maintenance requirements are found in the *Northeast Corridor 120-Day Preventive Maintenance Program Fiscal Year 2000* book. The book contains lists of tests, tasks, and inspections specified for the various maintenance personnel to follow for cleaning, repairing, and preparing cars for passenger service. A review of the 120-day maintenance book by Safety Board investigators revealed no requirement to ensure that appliances are secured and locked in place. The only appliance criterion was "disinfected, free of all food particles, grease, debris, and dirt inside, outside and underneath the appliance."

Personnel Information

The work/rest history, health, training, and experience of the CSXT freight traincrew, the CSXT dispatcher, and the Amtrak conductor were reviewed as part of this investigation. No potential problems were noted. The investigation focused on the Amtrak engineer, because he had the greatest influence over the events involving the accident.

Amtrak hired the engineer on April 16, 1986. He was originally hired by the former Penn Central Railroad (later Conrail) on June 17, 1970. His most recent engineer evaluation before the accident was on December 11, 2000. His evaluation report indicated that he met or exceeded Amtrak's requirements for skill and knowledge in all applicable performance categories, including operating rules compliance, signal compliance, train braking, and other train handling requirements. In the comment section of the report, the supervisor stated "nice job."

Amtrak Engineer 96-Hour History

The 49-year old Amtrak engineer said that he did not work on Friday, February 2, 2001. He awoke that day between about 11:15 and 11:30 a.m. and remained home. After eating supper, he watched some television and retired between 12:30 and 1:00 am Saturday, February 3.

He said he arose later on the morning of February 3 at 8:20 a.m. and reported for duty at 9:05 a.m. at his home terminal, the Albany Amtrak station. He took westbound Amtrak Train No. 63 from Albany to Syracuse and arrived at 1 p.m. He then went to the Amtrak-contracted motel for his short layover. He said that after washing up and having lunch, he went back to his room to watch television. He returned to the Syracuse station between 3:30 and 3:45 p.m. to work Amtrak Train No. 64 back to Albany.

He took Train No. 64 eastbound to Albany where he went off duty at 8:15 p.m. He went to bed about midnight and awoke at 9 a.m. the following morning, Sunday, February 4. He had breakfast, and later that day, at 4:35 p.m., he went on duty at the Albany station for westbound Amtrak train 283 with a scheduled departure of 5:30 pm.

Train No. 283 arrived in Syracuse between 8 and 8:10 p.m.. The engineer went off duty but boarded the train and continued on to Depew, New York, where he got off about 10:15 p.m. At Depew, he had dinner. He said he retired between 12:30 and 1 a.m. on Monday, February 5. He said he arose between 7:20 and 7:30 a.m. and had breakfast. The engineer then caught eastbound Amtrak train 286, the accident train, which arrived at the Depew Amtrak station and departed about 9:02 am. He arrived in Syracuse and took charge of the train at about 11:30 a.m. At the time of the accident, the Amtrak engineer had been awake for just over 4 hours and on duty for about 10 minutes

Training, Testing, Experience, and Discipline

According to the Amtrak superintendent, each Amtrak train crew supervisor is expected to conduct at least 100 efficiency tests[7] per quarter for rules compliance. Each efficiency test checks for compliance with one rule. It is common for an engineer to have multiple efficiency tests conducted on one occasion or during one testing visit from a supervisor. Each engineer, conductor, and assistant conductor is required to have at least one efficiency check per quarter. Engineers are required to receive a radar check (for speed compliance) each quarter and speed tape analysis every half year (for proper train handling).

Amtrak's efficiency-testing records for the Albany Division during the 11-month period, from January 31, 2000, to January 1, 2001, showed that a total of 952 tests were performed with 20 failures. Of the total, 718 tests were performed during daylight hours, and 234 were performed at night. Fifty of the tests were conducted on safety rules, 10 were banner rule tests,[8] and 892 tests were on operating rules.

Records revealed that the Amtrak engineer received the following training and testing:

Date	Training	Type	Result
4/1/99	Passenger Engineer	Recertification	Passed
4/15/99	Operating Rules	Annual	Passed
2/8/00	Operating Rules	Annual	Passed
9/28/00	Operating Rules	Annual	Passed

Between January 21, 1999, and December 9, 2000, the engineer of Amtrak train 286 received 49 efficiency tests and successfully passed them all. Of those tests, 28 (57 percent) were speed-related, including 10 compliance tests for indicated signal speeds. Of the 10 signal tests, 4 were for *medium approach* signal, one was for a *restricting* signal, one was for a *stop-and-proceed* signal, two were for *stop* signals, one was for an *approach* signal, and one was for a *clear* signal. The balance of the tests were on a variety of rules, including sign-ups and job briefings, train starting procedures, main track authority procedures, radio procedures, and air brake procedures.

Physical Health

Physical requirements for engineers are found at 49 CFR Part 240.121, which requires that engineers have a vision and auditory examination once every 3 years.[9] Both

---

[7] *Efficiency tests* are a method used by railroads to monitor and evaluate an employee's application, understanding, and compliance with the operating rules.

[8] The tested engineer is expected to stop the train short of a banner stretched across the track.

[9] CSXT requires engineer physicals every 3 years; Amtrak requires them annually.

contracted private and full-time railroad physicians perform engineer physical examinations. If an engineer fails to pass the examination, he may be re-examined or appeal for another examination by another doctor at a later date. Failure of the physical precludes train operation by the engineer.

Physical Examinations. Information pertaining to periodic physical examinations for Amtrak employees is found in a 15-page document dated July 11, 1989. According to this document, the purpose of the examinations is to "periodically evaluate the physical health of employees and determine their physical condition as related to safety and job performance." Periodic examinations are administered annually, regardless of the employee's age. Procedures address general vision, color vision, urinalysis to detect drugs and to determine protein and sugar levels, the cardiovascular system including electrocardiograms, hearing, height and weight, bones and joints, blood, blood forming organs, hernia, gastrointestinal, and genito-urinary systems, brain and nervous system, skin, respiratory exam, and tuberculin skin test. If elevated blood sugar levels are found, follow-up examinations and tests are performed to determine if medication is necessary. A determination is made later by Amtrak as to continuing fitness for duty.

Hyperglycemia.[10] As part of his routine annual evaluation by his cardiologist (the engineer had been treated for a heart attack in 1996), the engineer had blood tests performed which measured cholesterol and glucose (sugar) levels, among other assessments. Glucose levels were mildly elevated on three separate occasions, but there was no record of any assessment of these elevations. There was no indication in the cardiologist's records that the engineer had ever reported any symptoms of diabetes. Urine testing performed for annual railroad physical examinations was consistently negative for glucose, and the engineer did not report to Amtrak physicians that he had suffered any symptoms normally associated with diabetes.

During postaccident medical evaluations, the engineer told examining physicians that he had been experiencing symptoms of diabetes for several months preceding the accident. These reported symptoms included burning of his feet and increased thirst and urination. Four days after the accident, an ophthalmologist noted that the engineer stated his vision was stable. Five days later, an endocrinologist noted that the engineer had recently noted some blurred vision. The engineer said he did not note any symptoms of confusion before the accident, and he was described as alert and oriented in the emergency department of the hospital following the accident. Measured blood glucose level in the emergency department was 304 milligrams per deciliter (mg/dL) (normal values 70 to 110). Hemoglobin A1c measured on a blood specimen drawn on the day of the accident was 12.3 percent (normal values are less than 6 percent).

After the accident, and before he began any treatment for his diabetes, the engineer had two eye examinations, both of which were normal with the exception of a small amount of hyperopia (farsightedness) resulting in a mild decrease in visual acuity. No retinopathy was found on either examination. His worst uncorrected visual acuity before treatment was 20/40 in one eye on one occasion. In any case, his vision was correctable to

---

[10] Hyperglycemia is the technical term for elevated blood sugar.

20/20. This hyperopia did not resolve with treatment of his diabetes, though his worst uncorrected visual acuity improved to 20/25.

Train Information

After the accident, CSXT and Amtrak train crews were asked if they had any problems with their train's performance or equipment. All testified that their train equipment responded "normally," without any problems. No mechanical equipment problems were noted on any equipment defect forms located in the locomotive cabs. Safety Board investigators reviewed the maintenance records for all vehicles in the Amtrak train and the CSXT locomotive units. No mechanical equipment conditions or defects were found that would have precluded or hindered the designed operation of brakes or running gear or that would have affected train handling.

CSXT Train Q620

At the time of the collision, CSXT train Q620 consisted of two locomotive units pulling 92 freight cars (88 loads and 4 empties). Trailing tonnage was 9,640 tons. Train length was 6,002 feet. The freight train had a mixed consist of mostly paper and lumber. The train had originated in Montreal, Quebec, Canada, on February 4, 2001, and was interchanged to the CSXT at Massena, New York. It then moved south on the CSXT Montreal Secondary to Syracuse, where it entered the CSXT mainline at CP 291. The CSXT freight train moved east toward DeWitt Yard on the No. 1 main track. The train was destined for Selkirk, New York, near Albany.

As a result of the collision, the brake pipe on the last car was damaged. The freight train was then moved into DeWitt Yard, where the last car was cut out of the train and repaired. The rest of the train was inspected for damage, and the airbrake system was tested. Beyond the collision damage, no other air brake defects were found. No significant equipment anomalies or mechanical defects were found.

Amtrak Train 286

Amtrak train P286-05 had two locomotive units and five passenger cars. Locomotive 414 was the lead locomotive unit with the front in the direction of movement. Amtrak unit 411 was the second locomotive unit and also faced forward in the direction of movement. Both units were F40 model locomotives built by EMD (General Motors).

The passenger cars had various seating arrangements. The first passenger car, café car 48910, was designated as an Americans with Disabilities Act (ADA) car. The forward section of the car had business-class seating. The middle section of the car was the café/food service section, and the remaining section contained a table seating area. The second and third passenger cars, 21072 and 21250, were standard Amfleet I coaches that had 84 seats. The fourth passenger car, coach 21640, was a modified Amfleet I coach configured as an ADA coach with 74 seats. Modifications included the removal of 5 pairs of seats at the "A" end to accommodate an enlarged lavatory and a large open area forward of the seating area. The final car in the Amtrak consist was coach 21033, which was also a standard Amfleet I coach with 84 seats.

Before the Amtrak train was moved after the accident, the lead locomotive unit and passenger cars were rerailed and inspected for damage and repair estimates. There was no significant accumulation of snow or frozen precipitation on the brakes or running gear of the Amtrak train during postaccident inspection. The lead locomotive unit's electrical and air brake systems were isolated from the rest of the train. An initial terminal airbrake test using the second locomotive unit was performed under the supervision of Federal Railroad Administration (FRA), CSXT, and Amtrak representatives. All vehicles tested performed as designed. No mechanical or equipment conditions were found that would have affected the performance of the train.

Site Information

Track Configuration

The collision took place at MP 289.3[11] on the Albany Division of the Chicago Line of the CSXT Railroad.[12] The railroad in the vicinity of the accident consisted of four parallel tracks running east and west with the two middle tracks being the mainline tracks. Track designation from north to south was No. 8 runner, No. 1 main, No. 2 main, and No. 7 runner.

At CP 290 is an interlocking[13] with crossover tracks that allow trains to be routed from one track to another. CP 290 was placed in service during June 1998 to accommodate train movements for the newly constructed Syracuse Amtrak station.

As train 286 departed Syracuse eastbound toward CP-290, the train entered a 2,420-foot-long, 1-minute, 30-degree right-hand curve with no super-elevation and an ascending grade of 0.21 degrees.

Amtrak train 286 crossed over from track No. 7 to track No. 1 at CP-290. CP 290 is on tangent track with an ascending grade of 0.31 degrees. East of CP-290 is a 580-foot-long, 1-degree, 43-minute right-hand curve with a super-elevation of 3 inches and a 0.32-degree ascending grade. East of MP 290 is a 2,528-foot-long, 1-degree, 30-minute right-hand curve with a super-elevation of 2.5 inches and an ascending grade of 0.21 degrees. The point of impact between Amtrak train 286 and CSX Q620 was near MP 289.2,

---

[11] Mileposts are numbered according to their distance from New York City; consequently, mileposts numbers decrease in the eastbound direction.

[12] The railroad was originally part of the New York Central System Railroad from New York City to Chicago, Illinois; later Penn Central, and finally Conrail before becoming part of CSXT.

[13] An *interlocking* is an arrangement of signals and control apparatus so interconnected that functions must succeed each other in a predetermined sequence, thus permitting train movements along routes only if safe conditions exist.

approximately 12,807 feet east of the Syracuse Amtrak Station, on the spiral out, with approximately 1/16-inch super-elevation, 18 feet west of point of tangent and a continuation of the 0.21-degree ascending grade.

Track Maintenance

On the day of the accident, the No. 2 main track was taken out of service at about 9:37 a.m. in order to repair a switch component at CP 286. The repair was completed at about 11:50 a.m., 10 minutes after the collision. Postaccident inspection of CSXT track maintenance and repair records, and physical inspection of track in the accident area by Safety Board investigators and FRA inspectors, did not reveal any noteworthy track anomalies.

Signal System

Signal equipment consisted of Union Switch & Signal (US&S) color-light type signals, General Railway Signal (GRS) 120-volt d.c. Power-operated switch machines, and electronic and direct-control track circuits. A Vital Harmon Logic Controller (VHLC) controls CP 290. The VHLC is a solid-state application programmable controller designed to control wayside signals, switches, and track circuits at railroad interlocking plants.

The signal designated "6E" at the entrance to CP 290 used two US&S model CR-2 triangular color light signal heads mounted one above the other. (See figure 7.) Each of the two signal heads was mounted on a 36-inch-diameter circular background. The signal heads themselves consisted of a square housing with three 8 3/8-inch-diameter clear Lexan lenses in a triangular configuration. Behind each clear lens was a 5-inch-diameter colored lens of red, yellow, or green. Behind each of the three colored lenses was a GE SC-11 light bulb of a nominal 10 volts d.c. and 18 watts.

Figure 7. Close-up view of signal 6E. (Signal intensity not representative of actual appearance.)

Operations Information

Train Control

Train movement through the accident area is regulated by timetable and wayside signals that are part of a traffic control system (TCS) under the control of a CSXT dispatcher in Selkirk, New York. Mainline maximum authorized speed is 60 mph for passenger and intermodal trains,[14] and 50 mph for freight trains. Speed limits for diverging movements over turnouts[15] and crossovers are slower. The turn outs at CP 290 were designed for a maximum speed of 30 mph.

Part of the dispatcher's job is to align routes for trains through his territory. The dispatcher aligns train routes through the interlockings by first setting turnout switches and then setting the corresponding signals for speed and route. If the dispatcher attempts to align a switch for a conflicting or unsafe route that could cause a collision, the system will not allow the switch to be set and forces the dispatcher to select another route or to stop a train to wait until the route is clear.

In order for an eastbound Amtrak train to stop at the Syracuse Amtrak station, the train must move from either the No. 1 or No. 2 main track to the No. 7 track via crossover switches at CP 291. Both main tracks are signaled for movement in either direction, east or west. Eastbound Amtrak train 286 received authority from the dispatcher to proceed on the No. 7 track to arrive at Syracuse station on signal indication at CP 291 from the No. 2 main track.

Train Traffic

According to the CSXT superintendent, track repairs in and around DeWitt Yard are usually performed on Mondays, when train traffic is lightest and service interruptions are minimal. Traffic density through the accident area is about 5 trains per hour. This includes a daily average of 8 passenger trains. Traffic volume is about 80 million gross tons per year.

As previously mentioned, on the day of the accident, No. 2 main track was taken out of service at about 9:37 a.m. so that repairs could be made near CP 286. This left only the No. 1 main track available to route eastbound trains from CP 290 through CP 286 into or around DeWitt Yard, and the dispatcher had fleeted, or lined up, trains to follow one another on that track. A yard local and three freight trains (the last being Q620) had been routed onto main track No. 1 ahead of Amtrak train 286.

CSXT train Q620 was a through train that did not have to be switched at DeWitt Yard, but the train did have to stop for a crew change. The dispatcher had decided to route

---

[14] *Intermodal trains* are freight trains carrying truck trailers and intermodal containers.

[15] A *turnout* is a part of the railroad track structure that allows the rolling equipment to move onto another track. The *switch* is the moveable part of the turnout. Turnouts are commonly called switches. Two opposing turnouts make a crossover between parallel tracks.

Q620 into a control siding at CP 285 for the crew change at CP 283 rather than block the mainline. He planned to route Amtrak train 286 around Q620 at that point.

CSXT train Q620 entered CP290 at 11:09 a.m. and was through that control point at 11:22 a.m. About 11:34 a.m., train Q620 had stopped for a *stop and proceed* signal at the automatic signal at MP 287. Shortly after Q620 started moving again, the freight engineer made a distress call to the dispatcher at 11:39:47 a.m. at MP 287 and reported that his train was in emergency (having been struck by the following Amtrak train). The freight train had been moving about 7 mph when the emergency occurred.

When the Amtrak engineer was asked how often he had been required to follow a freight train that was routed past or into DeWitt Yard, he replied, "The dispatchers usually keep you moving. I would say in this last year I might have followed three freight trains." He also said that if he did "get stuck" behind a freight train, it was usually further east, around MP 283.

Lone-Engineer Operation

General. The Amtrak engineer was operating by himself in the locomotive control cab at the time of the accident. One- or lone-engineer operation is common in Amtrak operations nationwide. On the Northeast Corridor between Washington, D.C., and Boston, a positive train control system provides a level of safety redundancy in the event the engineer is incapacitated or fails to take appropriate action in response to a signal. With this system, if the engineer fails to comply with a more restrictive signal, the train is automatically brought to a stop by a penalty application of the brakes. No fail-safe positive train control system was in operation at the site of this accident.

All Amtrak intercity locomotive cabs, such as the one involved in the accident, are equipped with alerters.[16] Most alerters are electronic or electro-mechanical devices that provide audible and visual warnings if the engineer fails, within a specified time period, to touch certain metal objects and/or to make a control manipulation, such as a throttle or brake adjustment. The specified time interval varies with the speed of the locomotive: the faster the speed, the shorter the time interval between required movements. According to Amtrak, locomotive alerters help ensure that lone-engineer operation is safe even in the absence of positive train control or other backup safety systems.

History. The routine operation of intercity trains by an engineer who is alone in the cab began on passenger trains in the Northeast Corridor by the then Penn Central Railroad in the 1960s. Amtrak inherited Metroliner lone-engineer operation on the Northeast Corridor when Amtrak was created on May 1, 1971. In 1983, Amtrak expanded lone-engineer operation to all passenger trains on the Northeast Corridor and began lone-engineer operation on trains outside the Northeast Corridor. Until 1998, Amtrak operated under a collective bargaining agreement rule that required two engineers (an engineer and an assistant engineer) if the duration of the run was scheduled to be more than 4 hours. For

---

[16] Alerters are used to help ensure that the engineer is alert and as a fatigue countermeasure.

scheduled runs under 4 hours, only a single engineer was required. This was called the "4-hour rule."

In 1997, in order to reduce Amtrak operating costs, collective bargaining concessions were made by the unions, such as the Brotherhood of Locomotive Engineers (BLE), that represented Amtrak employees. The BLE and Amtrak agreed to expand the 4-hour rule to a new 6-hour rule that would allow lone-engineer operation if the scheduled run of the train was 6 hours or less. The new rule became effective on August 1, 1998.

The FRA and Lone-Engineer Operations. According to the manager of the FRA's Amtrak safety assurance and compliance program, in 1998, the BLE expressed concerns to the FRA about Amtrak's one-person train operation between Spokane, Washington, and Whitefish, Montana. The concern was about lone engineers operating at night in an area subject to severe weather without a system, such as cab signals or positive train control, to provide safety backup.

The FRA brought these concerns to the attention of Amtrak, and a meeting was held in November 1998. The meeting was attended by representatives of the BLE, Amtrak, and Circadian Technologies, Inc., who had been invited by Amtrak. Circadian Technologies representatives made a presentation on locomotive engineer fatigue as it affects alertness. The FRA expressed particular concern about lone-engineer operation between midnight and 6 a.m., when the risk of fatigue appeared to be greatest. In response to the FRA's concern, Amtrak identified 39 assignments that had a 3-hour or more intrusion into the midnight-to-6-a.m. time period and committed to placing a second person in the cab of the locomotive for those 39 assignments.

Canadian Action. The Transportation Safety Board of Canada recently published its report of an accident investigation involving one-person, or lone-engineer, operation that, like the Syracuse accident, was also a rear-end collision through a restricting signal.[17]

According to the report, on July 14, 1996, about 10:45 a.m., a Quebec North Shore and Labrador Railway (QNS&L)[18] southbound freight train collided with the rear end of a stationary freight train at Mile 131.68 of the Wacouna Subdivision. The last three rail cars of the stationary train derailed and were extensively damaged. The lead locomotive unit of the moving train was extensively damaged. The locomotive engineer of the moving train sustained minor injuries.

The report of the accident concluded, among other things:

- There was no other railway employee in a position to question the actions taken by the locomotive engineer;

---

[17] Transportation Safety Board of Canada, Report No. R96Q0050, and *Reflexions*, Issue 17, Winter 2001.

[18] The QNS&L runs between the St. Lawrence port at Sept Isle, Quebec, north though Labrador to the site of the now closed Schefferville, Quebec, iron mine. The line comprises 357 track miles (260 road miles). A 37-mile-long branch line located 224 miles north of Sept Iles, at Ross Bay Junction, runs to Labrador City, where mining operations continue.

- The possibility that fatigue may have contributed to the locomotive engineer's decision not to comply with the governing signal indication cannot be ignored;

- Locomotive-engineer-only train operations were implemented on the QNS&L without the benefit of a comprehensive analysis of the impact a further crew reduction would have on their operation and without the introduction of countermeasures that would ensure an equivalent level of safety.

The Transportation Safety Board of Canada determined that the collision occurred because:

> The moving train was operated past a governing restrictive signal at a speed at which the locomotive engineer was unable to stop short of the stationary equipment. The implementation of the major operational change to locomotive-engineer-only train operation without a comprehensive analysis of its impact and without the implementation of effective compensatory safety measures contributed to this occurrence.

After the accident, Transport Canada[19] prohibited the railway from operating trains with only a locomotive engineer until the railway had received appropriate exemptions from the Canadian Rail operating rules. Transport Canada stipulated 13 specific safety-related conditions (including the bulleted items below) that had to be met before the exemptions could be granted. The railway met the conditions, and appropriate exemptions were granted on April 24, 1997.

As a result of the Canadian investigation, a working group was established comprising Transport Canada staff and representatives of the QNS&L Railway and the United Transportation Union. The working group outlined more than 65 needed improvements, to include the following:

- The installation and operation of a proximity detection device on all lead locomotive units, track units, and on-track vehicles operating on main line track;

- Increased supervision;

- More intensive engineer training, including 120 to 130 hours of simulator training, first aid, fire extinguisher use, proper interpretation and application of the rules, proper use of the proximity detection device system, and applicable emergency procedures;

- A requirement that the railway implement and maintain an engineer performance record data system with indicators and tracking mechanisms;

- Specialized training of dispatchers working with lone engineers;

- Specialized training of supervisors of lone engineers;

---

[19] Transport Canada is the Canadian equivalent of the FRA.

- Additional fatigue mitigation training and practices, including:
  Implementation of crew calling windows;
  Recognized and scheduled rest periods; and
  Specific time off.

- Lone-engineer checklists and standard operating procedures;

- Required cab conditions;

- A requirement to call signals over the radio;

- Specified radio procedures and practices;

- Provision of feedback mechanisms for engineers; and

- Additional emergency procedures.

After the Canadian accident, Transport Canada commissioned a study[20] of one-person train operations. The Canadian study found that many foreign railroads employed lone-engineer operation, but that all had some degree of safety redundancy built in, either with equipment and/or training and supervision. The Canadian study concluded that "all railways found the one-person safety record to be excellent and do not believe that two persons in the cab improves safety. The drivers [engineers] were initially opposed to the concept but the system now has gained wide acceptance."

Currently in Canada, only the QNS&L Railway has been approved for lone-engineer operation; however, Transport Canada has indicated it will consider lone-engineer operation on a waiver basis for other Canadian railroads as long as certain conditions are met.

Meteorological Information

The closest official weather reporting facility to the accident site was Syracuse Hancock International Airport, about 4 miles southeast of Syracuse. The airport is equipped with a Federal automated surface observing system and is also augmented by National Weather Service-certified observers. The following weather conditions were reported surrounding the time of the accident:

At 10:54 a.m. EST: wind was from 050 degrees at 6 knots, visibility 7 miles in light snow, ceiling broken at 2,800 feet, overcast at 3,400 feet, temperature 30 °F, dew point 25 °F. Remarks: snow began at 10:30 a.m. EST; precipitation since last hour less than 0.01 inch.

Weather observation at 11:47 a.m. EST: wind from 090 degrees at 7 knots, visibility 3 statute miles in light snow and mist, ceiling overcast at 3,400 feet, temperature

---

[20] Transport Canada, TP 12974E, "Study of One-Person Train Operations," Beauchemin-Beaton-Lapointe Inc., 1997.

30 °F, dew point 27 °F). Remarks: precipitation reported since last hour less than 0.01 inches.

The total snow depth reported on the ground at 6:00 a.m. and at 1:00 p.m. EST was 4 inches, with no new snow accumulation reported during the period.

Toxicological Information

The CSXT engineer and conductor and the engineer of the Amtrak train were toxicologically tested about 5 hours after the accident in accordance with 49 CFR Part 219 Subpart C at St. Joseph's Hospital/Health Center, in Syracuse, New York. Each provided blood and urine specimens that were tested for alcohol and other drugs. The results were negative for all the tested employees.

Additionally, blood and urine specimens that were obtained from the Amtrak engineer as part of his postaccident medical evaluation were obtained by the Safety Board for independent toxicological analysis at the Civil Aeromedical Institute (CAMI) in Oklahoma City, Oklahoma. The results were negative for the presence of alcohol and drugs.

Disaster Preparedness

The chief of the Lyncourt Fire Department assumed incident command according to Section III of the *Onondaga County Comprehensive Emergency Management Plan*. Officials told the Safety Board that the command and control portions of the plan had been practiced on several occasions before the accident. In May 2000, Onondaga County conducted a mass casualty exercise that simulated an airplane crash involving 43 casualties plus 18 fatalities. In September 2000, Onondaga County conducted hazardous materials training with the CSXT. No previous training had been done with regard to passenger trains with or without Amtrak or CSXT. Amtrak does provide passenger train equipment and locomotives, along with an instructor, to the New York State Association of Fire Chief's annual conference, which is held in Syracuse.

Tests and Research

Sight Distance Test

Sight distance tests were conducted between 11:30 a.m. and 1:30 p.m. 2 days after the collision on February 7, 2001. The purpose of the tests was to determine (1) at what distance signal 6E at CP 290 may have been visible to the Amtrak engineer and, (2) at what distance along track No. 1 an engineer could see the end of a freight train ahead and determine that it was on the same track. The tests were conducted under conditions similar to those existing at the time of the accident. The tests were made at the same time of day, in similar weather and lighting conditions, and using the same model Amtrak locomotive and the same track and operating conditions as recorded and/or described by the Amtrak engineer and other witnesses.

The signal sight distance test started from the Syracuse Amtrak station. Signal observations were made from the station to signal 6E, about 3,688 feet away. The last 1,364 feet of this distance is in a 1-degree, 30-minute, curve. The signal was initially activated with a *restricting* indication (steady or solid red light over a solid yellow light), and then with a *medium approach* indication (solid red light over a flashing yellow light). All test observers reported being able to clearly see both the *restricting* and the *medium approach* signals about 898 feet before the signal. Test observers also noted that the flashing yellow light was distinct and easily recognizable when compared to the solid yellow light.

For the second sight distance test, a bulkhead flat car, similar to the one that had been on the end of the struck CSXT freight train, was positioned at the point-of-impact on the No. 1 main track.[21] The test observers reported that the rear of the freight car could be clearly seen and recognized as on the No. 1 main track from a distance of 1,054 feet.

Signal Tests

After the accident, the bulb for the red display on the top signal head of signal 6E (which was lighted at the time Amtrak train 286 passed the signal) was measured at 9.6 volts d.c. The bulb for the yellow display of the bottom signal head (lighted for train 286) was measured at 9.4 volts d.c. The flasher relay that causes a signal bulb to flash for certain signal aspects was found to be working as designed.

Safety Board investigators examined the test records, field memory logs, and office diagnostic logs of signal, switch, and train movements. Site inspections and tests were conducted at CP 290 to verify train movements and signal aspects displayed. Testing included a fault tree analysis matrix of recommended manufacturer simulations to ensure the integrity of the signal system. Aspect charts were examined to determine what signal aspects would be displayed at CP 290 for several selected routes. No exceptions were taken to the operation of the signal system. All inspections and tests determined that signal 6E at CP 290 displayed, and could only display, a *restricting* (solid red over solid yellow) aspect for the route alignment and track occupancies at the time of the accident.

Amtrak Stopping Distance Information

At the request of the Safety Board, Amtrak provided calculated stopping distances for the accident train. Safety Board investigators compared these stopping distances with specified braking distances for Amtrak equipment and previous accident braking tests

---

[21] Since the CSXT freight train was moving about 7 mph (10 feet per second) at the time the Amtrak engineer saw the end of the freight train, the actual distance traveled by the Amtrak train before impact exceeded the initial sight distance of the Amtrak engineer.

with similar Amtrak equipment. These calculations are based on level, straight track with clean dry rail at the speeds indicated:

Amtrak Stopping Distances (in feet)

Braking Mode	Speed		
	15 mph	30 mph	57 mph
Full Service	168	513	1,637
Emergency	119	392	1,275

Other Information

Event Recorder Information

Both Amtrak locomotive units were equipped with Bach Simpson TMACS solid-state event recorders, model TMACS 100. Although both locomotive units had the same model of recorder, the data sampling methods were different. The lead locomotive recorder recorded data whenever there was an event change, such as a change in train speed of at least 2 mph, a change in brake pipe pressure of at least 5 psi, a change in voltage of at least 10 volts, or a change in traction motor current of at least 50 amps. The trailing locomotive recorder sampled and recorded data once every 3 seconds, irrespective of event changes. Both recorders rounded data to the nearest whole integer. The Safety Board inputted time as it corresponded to recorded wayside signal and dispatching times. The Bach Simpson event recorder readout software used for the Amtrak data does not calculate distance traveled; therefore, distance traveled was derived from the time and wheel speed data.

Analysis

The Accident

When Amtrak train 286 departed the Syracuse station, it was to take its place behind several other trains on the only available mainline track–track No. 1. As a way of expediting train movements despite the dense traffic, the dispatcher was using restrictive signals to permit trains to follow one another at relatively close intervals. The restrictive signals required locomotive engineers to progress at restricted speed while looking out for the rear of the train ahead.

As Amtrak train 286 approached the interlocking at CP 290, the dispatcher had set signal 6E as *restricting*, indicating that the engineer should (1) slow his train to a speed no greater than 15 mph that would allow him to stop within half his sight distance, and (2) be on the alert for trains or other obstructions on the track ahead.

But the Amtrak engineer stated that he thought the signal indication was *medium approach*, requiring that he slow to 30 mph and be prepared to stop at the next signal. By implication, a *medium approach* signal indication signifies that the block immediately ahead is clear of other trains and that the engineer need only be concerned about the possibility of a train in the block controlled by the next signal.

Shortly after the Amtrak train passed signal 6E, the engineer activated a switch that effectively doubled the motive power being applied to the train, and the train's speed began to increase. The engineer said that he then took his eyes off the track ahead and began going through his bag for track bulletins. While he did so, the train's speed continued to increase well past either restricted or medium approach speed. The engineer said that the distraction of retrieving bulletins (which he could, and should, have retrieved and placed in an accessible location before he departed the Syracuse station) from his bag prevented his noticing the speed increase.

Meanwhile, CSXT freight train Q620, which was immediately in front of the Amtrak train, had reached a speed of 7 mph after having stopped for a *stop and proceed* signal indication. The Amtrak engineer said that he looked up to see the rear of the freight train ahead. By that time, the Amtrak train had reached a speed of about 59 mph. The engineer said that once he determined that the train was on the same track, he placed the train in emergency, but it was not able to stop before striking the rear of CSXT train Q620. The Amtrak train was traveling about 35 mph when it struck the rear of the freight train.

The safety issues addressed in the report are as follows:

- The lack of a positive train control system to prevent train collisions;
- The adequacy of Amtrak's procedures for ensuring that appliances on Amtrak trains are always properly secured.

- The adequacy of maps used by emergency response personnel for railroad accidents.

The investigation also addressed the pinpointing of accident locations for emergency response.

Exclusions

Weather

Safety Board investigators examined if the weather conditions may have impaired the engineer's ability to see the signal, and if precipitation may have affected the braking ability of the train. Although light snow was falling at the time of the collision, the CSXT conductor said visibility was not reduced. The Amtrak engineer also said his ability to see was uninhibited and recalled the weather as "clear." When sight distance tests were performed 2 days after the accident under similar weather conditions, participants had no difficulty seeing or identifying the signal aspects. The official weather service reports recorded visibility at 3 miles or more.

The recorded total snow depth of 4 inches was well below the top of the rail, and no significant accumulation of snow or frozen precipitation was found on the brakes or running gear of the Amtrak train during postaccident inspection. The rail on the No. 1 main track had just been cleaned by the recent passage of the struck CSXT freight train, and neither the Amtrak inbound nor the Amtrak accident engineer said that they had any braking problems related to precipitation or the weather. The Safety Board therefore concludes that weather was not causal or contributory to the accident.

Track and Signals

CSXT track inspectors inspected the track through the accident area before the collision on the day of the accident. No exceptions were noted. The track structure remained relatively undisturbed after the accident. Safety Board investigators conducted a postaccident review of the track inspection records and the track through the accident area, and no exceptions were noted.

Since the track structure was relatively undisturbed after the accident, the integrity of the signal system had been maintained. The signal system was tested, and each part of the system worked as designed. All inspections and tests determined that signal 6E at CP-290 displayed, and could only display, a *restricting* (solid red over solid yellow) aspect for the route alignment and track occupancies at the time of the accident. Therefore the Safety Board concludes that the wayside signal, before the accident, displayed a *restricting* aspect and functioned as designed.

Toxicology

Toxicological tests were performed after the accident on the CSXT engineer and conductor, and the Amtrak engineer; no evidence of alcohol or drug use was found.

Fatigue

Safety Board investigators examined the work-rest cycle and 96-hour history of the Amtrak engineer. During his interview conducted on April 10, 2001, the Amtrak engineer reported that he obtained 6 to 7 hours of sleep during his off-duty time the day before the accident. He also reported that he felt fine on the morning of the accident. The Amtrak engineer had boarded the accident train at about 9:00 a.m. at Depew and had relaxed on the train before taking charge of the train at 11:30. He had been on duty for only about 10 minutes when the accident occurred. Therefore, the Safety Board concludes that crewmember fatigue likely was not a factor in the accident, and that drugs or alcohol did not cause or contribute to the accident.

Equipment

Both CSXT and Amtrak train crews testified that their trains responded "normally," as expected, without any problems. No mechanical equipment problems were noted on any equipment defect forms located in the locomotive cabs. The Safety Board's postaccident review of the maintenance records for all vehicles in the Amtrak train and the CSXT locomotive units did not reveal any conditions or defects that might have caused or contributed to the collision. No significant equipment anomalies or mechanical defects were found that would have caused or contributed to the collision. Considering accident damage, all equipment performed as designed during postaccident testing. Therefore the Safety Board concludes that neither of the trains involved in this accident had a mechanical condition that caused or contributed to the collision.

Amtrak Engineer Physical Condition

On the day of the accident, the engineer's blood sugar had been measured as significantly above normal. This measurement had been made when the engineer was taken to the hospital shortly after the collision. Investigators questioned whether the engineer's physical condition may have affected his cognitive ability and/or his vision and whether this may have affected his ability to see and correctly identify signal 6E at CP 290.

Several studies have been performed that measure blood glucose in newly diagnosed non-insulin-dependent diabetics at various times of day.[22] Review of these studies indicates that untreated non-insulin-dependent diabetics increase their blood glucose levels to a peak approximately 2 hours following a meal or a high glucose-content beverage. This peak is consistently less than 200 mg/dL over the fasting blood glucose levels and falls to less than 100 mg/dL above fasting levels by 4 hours after the meal. According to the engineer, he had breakfast about 4 hours before the accident. It is reasonable to conclude that his blood glucose level would have been dropping at the time of the accident and that it would have been no more than 100 mg/dL above his fasting blood glucose level. Although the engineer's fasting blood glucose level is not known, it would represent the lowest level of blood glucose that he experienced during the day, and would therefore be expected to be significantly lower than his calculated average of approximately 325-350 mg/dL. It would thus be most likely that his blood glucose level at the time of the accident would be near his average, and extremely unlikely that it would have exceeded 400 mg/dL.

Additionally, hormones (notably cortisol and corticotropin) that are secreted normally in response to physical or emotional stress tend to significantly elevate blood glucose even in non-diabetics.[23] Stress can thus lead to substantial blood glucose elevations for a considerable period of time. It is therefore reasonable to expect that the engineer's blood glucose would have risen in response to stress in the 4 1/2 hours following the accident before his blood was drawn in the emergency department. The value of 304 mg/dL measured in the emergency department may have been higher than the actual value at the time of the accident.

Diabetes is well known to result in long-term damage to the retina, termed diabetic retinopathy. Substantial changes in blood glucose are also known to result in changes in refraction (the ability of the eye to focus images accurately) due to a temporary thickening of the lens.[24] Before he began any postaccident treatment for his diabetes, the engineer had had two eye examinations, both of which were normal with the exception of a small amount of farsightedness. This farsightedness did not resolve with treatment of his diabetes, though his worst uncorrected visual acuity improved to 20/25, suggesting an improved ability to compensate for his farsightedness as his lens returned to normal. The thickening of the lens expected from the engineer's elevated blood glucose likely interfered with his ability to accommodate (to change the shape of his lens to correctly focus images); however, his distant visual acuity 5 days after the accident without correction or treatment would not have been disqualifying, even without correction. While the engineer may have had some fluctuations in his visual acuity at the time of the accident, it is unlikely that such fluctuations rendered him unable to correctly perceive the signal aspect. At worst, the signal would have been somewhat blurrier than usual.

---

[22] See, for example: (a) Mooy J.M.; Grootenhuis, P.A.; de Vries, H,.; and others. 1996. "Intra-individual Variation of Glucose, Specific Insulin and Proinsulin Concentrations Measured by Two Oral Glucose Tolerance Tests in a General Caucasian Population: the Hoorn Study." *Diabetologia*. 39(3):298-305, (b) Owens D.R.; Dolben, J.; Jones I.R.; and others. 1989. "Hormonal and glycaemic responses to serial meals in newly diagnosed non insulin dependent diabetic patients." *Diabete and Metabolisme* 15(1):1-4. (c) Coate, P.A.; Ollerton, R.L.; Luzio, S.D., and others. 1994 "A glimpse of the 'natural history' of established type 2 (non-insulin dependent) diabetes mellitus from the spectrum of metabolic and hormonal responses to a mixed meal at the time of diagnosis." *Diabetes Research and Clinical Practice* 26(3):177-87, (d) Atiea, J.A.; Vora, J.P.; Owens, D.R., and others. 1988. "Non-insulin-dependent diabetic patients (NIDDMs) do not demonstrate the dawn phenomenon at presentation." *Diabetes Research and Clinical Practice* 5(1):37-44, and (e) Ollerton, R.L.; Playle, R.; Ahmed, K., and others. 1999. "Day-to-day variability of fasting plasma glucose in newly diagnosed type 2 diabetic subjects." *Diabetes Care* 22(3):394-8.

[23] Williams, G.H. and Dluhy, R.G.. 1994. "Diseases of the Adrenal Cortex." In: Isselbacher, K.J.; Braunwals, E.,;Wilson, J.D.; Martin; J.B.; Fauci, A.S.; Kasper, D.L., eds. *Harrision's Principles of Internal Medicine*. McGraw Hill, Inc., New York.. pp. 1979-2000.

[24] Furushima, M; Imaizumi, M; Nakatsuka, K. 1999. "Changes in refraction caused by induction of acute hyperglycemia in healthy volunteers." *Japanese Journal of Ophthalmology* 43(5):398-403.

A recent study of the cognitive function of 34- to 65-year-old non-insulin-dependent diabetics who had been diagnosed for at least 2 years indicated that they did not suffer from any deficits in learning, memory, or problem-solving skills, though they did perform more slowly on some psychomotor tasks, performance which was worse with poorer control of diabetes.[25] A similar study performed on older patients revealed that the diabetics performed more poorly on measures of verbal learning, abstract reasoning, and complex psychomotor functions, though there were no deficits in pure motor speed or simple verbal tasks.[26] The general conclusion that can be drawn from the articles referenced is that, while there may have been some subtle effects of the engineer's diabetes on his performance, the performance of a highly learned task, such as correctly responding to a familiar signal aspect, should not have been substantially impaired. Of importance, the engineer's alertness and general cognitive function appeared normal to investigators and treating physicians on the day of the accident.

In general, though the engineer might have been suffering from some minor visual changes and even some mild cognitive dysfunction as a result of his unrecognized and untreated diabetes, these impairments would not be sufficient to explain his response to the displayed signal aspect at the time he passed it. Therefore, the Safety Board concludes that the physical condition of the engineer at the time of the accident did not significantly affect his ability to perceive and appropriately respond to the wayside signals or properly control the train.

Actions of the Amtrak Engineer

Because no track, signal, or equipment factors were found that could have caused or contributed to the accident, the investigation focused on the actions of the Amtrak engineer and the fact that he was operating alone without any redundant safety system to help prevent a collision. The investigation attempted to determine the possible reasons the engineer failed to comply with the signal at CP 290 and subsequently failed to stop before striking the CSXT train.

Expectation

The Amtrak engineer told Safety Board investigators that in his experience, it was rare to be routed close behind a freight train, and that when it did happen, it was usually farther east than CP 290. He said that he had never gotten a *restricting* signal (solid red over solid yellow) at CP 290. He said that he got a *medium approach* (solid red over flashing yellow) only about 40 percent of the time and that the most common signal was *clear* (actually *medium clear*, or red over green). Therefore, the engineer did not expect a *restricting* signal; he expected, based on his experience, either (*medium*) *clear* or *medium*

---

[25] Ryan, C.M., and Geckle, M.O. 2000. "Circumscribed cognitive dysfunction in middle-aged adults with type 2 diabetes." *Diabetes Care* 23(10):1486-93.

[26] Reaven, G.M.; Thompson, L.W.; Nahum, D.; Haskins, E. 1990 "Relationship between hyperglycemia and cognitive function in older NIDDM patients" *Diabetes Care* 13(1):16-21.

approach. When the engineer saw a red over a yellow signal, it most closely matched his expectation of a *medium approach* aspect. Consequently, the engineer either saw what he expected to see, rather than what the signal actually displayed, or he never saw the signal.

Distraction

After the engineer misidentified the signal, he compounded the error by failing to comply with the requirements not only of the actual signal indication, but also of the signal he believed he saw. The *medium approach* indication the engineer said he believed he saw would have required that he operate his train at no more than 30 mph. In fact, data recorder information showed that the train was traveling only 28 mph when it passed signal 6E. But shortly thereafter, the engineer said, he became involved in activities that caused him to take his eyes off the tracks ahead and divert his attention from controlling the train.

According to the event recorder, the engineer turned the isolation switch on the back wall of the locomotive cab to "Run" after the head-end of the train had passed the signal at CP 290, somewhere between 7,430 and 7,934 feet from the collision point. In order to turn the isolation switch, the engineer had to get up out of his seat and redirect his attention. Shortly after sitting down again, the engineer said that he became involved in another distraction when he began to look for his bulletins. At the time, the throttle was in the eighth notch–the highest setting. At one point, the train speed reached 59 mph, almost double the speed authorized by the signal indication that the engineer said that he saw.

Based on postaccident sight distance tests, the rear end of freight train Q620 was clearly visible from a distance of 1,054 feet. The engineer placed the train in emergency about 841 feet from the freight train. The calculated stopping distance for the accident train, at 30 mph, was 513 feet for full-service braking and 392 feet for emergency. Both these distances are well within the 841 feet within which the Amtrak train attempted to stop. The Safety Board therefore concludes that had the Amtrak train been traveling at either the actual authorized *restricted* speed of 15 mph or less, or at the Amtrak engineer's perceived *medium approach* maximum speed of 30 mph, the Amtrak engineer would have been able to stop short of the freight train.

Positive Train Control

The Safety Board is concerned about the safety of passenger train service when the train is being operated by a lone engineer and backup systems are not available to intervene if the engineer operates his train improperly or fails to comply with wayside signals. The Safety Board has long argued that the most effective way to avoid train-to-train collisions–regardless of the number of persons in the operating compartment–is through the use of positive train control systems. Such systems prevent train collisions by automatically assuming some control of the train when the engineer does not comply with the requirements of the signal indication. Although the signals in the area of the accident were operating properly, the train control system did not include any mechanism to help make the engineer aware of signal indications and did not incorporate safeguards to prevent the engineer from accidentally or intentionally failing to comply with restrictive signals.

Most Amtrak locomotives, including the lead locomotive on Amtrak train 286, have automatic cab signal equipment that is designed to display signal indications inside the locomotive cab. However, the track in the accident area was not equipped with the wayside equipment to transmit signal information to the locomotive, although such equipment was installed much further east, starting at MP 169 outside Schenectady, New York. Had there been a functioning cab signal system in place in the accident area, the restrictive signal in this accident would have been displayed inside the cab of the lead Amtrak locomotive unit 414, where it might have been observed correctly and properly responded to by the engineer.

At one time, the Chicago main line through the accident area was equipped with an intermittent automatic train stop system that was designed to automatically apply the air brakes and stop the train should the engineer fail to acknowledge an audible alarm within a few seconds of passing a more restrictive wayside signal. This feature, however, was removed with the approval of the FRA in the early 1970s after the Penn Central Railroad was created from the merger of the Pennsylvania and New York Central Railroads.[27]

Even though a working automatic cab signal or automatic train stop system might have helped prevent this accident, the Safety Board notes that these systems, too, rely for their effectiveness on the alertness, judgment, and responsiveness of the train crew. For example, the automatic cab signal system displays signal indications but does nothing to ensure that the crew responds appropriately. Similarly, the automatic train stop system, while offering a level of safety beyond that of cab signals, does not enforce compliance with restrictive signal indications. So long as the engineer pushes a button or turns a lever to acknowledge and silence the system alarm, the automatic stop system will not activate.

The Safety Board has long been a proponent of automated systems that prevent train collisions by automatically interceding in the operation of a train when the engineer does not comply with the requirements of the signal indication.[28] Had Amtrak train 286 been equipped with such a system, the system would have intervened by slowing the train when the train engineer failed to slow in response to passing the *restricting* signal indication, whether or not the engineer misinterpreted or missed seeing the signal. The Safety Board concludes that had a fail-safe safety redundancy system such as positive train control been installed and operational throughout the accident area, the accident would probably not have occurred.

---

[27] Automatic train stop was installed by the New York Central System railroad through the accident area from Croton, New York, to Englewood, Illinois, between 1922 and 1934.

[28] For a more detailed discussion of Safety Board activities in the area of positive train control, see National Transportation Safety Board, *Collision Involving Three Consolidated Rail Corporation Freight Trains Operating in Fog at Bryan, Ohio, January 17, 1999*, Railroad Accident Report RAR-01/01 (Washington, D.C.: NTSB, 2001).

In 1996, the Safety Board investigated the February 16, 1996, accident in Silver Spring, Maryland, in which the crew of a Maryland Rail Commuter (MARC) train did not comply with signal indications and collided with an Amtrak passenger train.[29] The collision, derailment, and subsequent fire killed 11 people, including the entire MARC train crew, and injured 26 other people. As a result of its investigation of the Silver Spring accident, the Board issued the following safety recommendation to the CSXT:

R-97-26

Develop and install a positive train separation [PTS] control system on track segments that have commuter and intercity passenger trains.

In a December 12, 1997, response to this safety recommendation, the CSXT asserted its commitment to the development of positive train control systems and stated that it was actively supporting the development of a state-of-the-art system. In an October 7, 1998, follow-up letter to the Safety Board, the CSXT stated that research and development of an open architecture design specification was complete and that the development of positive train control systems had moved to the procurement stage with a goal of an interoperable/compatible platform aboard locomotives. Based on these responses, the Safety Board classified Safety Recommendation R-97-26 "Open–Acceptable Response." The Safety Board is currently seeking an update of CSXT progress in the development and deployment of positive train control.

Also as a result of its investigation of the Silver Spring accident, the Safety Board made the following safety recommendation to the FRA:

R-97-12

Require, in the interim of a positive train separation control system being available, the installation of cab signals, automatic train stop, automatic train control, or other similar redundant systems for all trains where commuter and intercity passengers railroads operate.

In a February 25, 1998, letter in response to Safety Recommendation R-97-12, the FRA stated that it was

> pressing for implementation of [positive train control] and similar systems that are reasonable taking into consideration the mix of traffic, division of benefits flowing from the systems, opportunities for interoperability of onboard equipment, and the readiness of available technology.

Because the FRA was not responsive to requiring alternate redundant systems and had instead chosen to wait for a more fully developed positive train control system, the Safety Board classified Safety Recommendation R-97-12 "Closed–Unacceptable Action."

---

[29] National Transportation Safety Board, *Collision and Derailment of Maryland Rail Commuter MARC Train 286 and National Railroad Passenger Corporation (Amtrak) Train 29 Near Silver Spring, Maryland, February 16, 1996*, Railroad Accident Report RAR-97-02 (Washington, D.C.: NTSB, 1997).

The most recent positive train control safety recommendation issued by the Safety Board came as a result of the Board's investigation of a January 17, 1999, train collision in Bryan, Ohio.[30] In that accident, a freight train locomotive crew, operating in dense fog, failed to see and appropriately respond to two restrictive signal indications. As a result, the train struck the rear of a slower moving freight train. The derailed equipment also struck and caused the derailment of some cars of a passing train on an adjacent track. As a result of the investigation of the Bryan, Ohio, accident, the Safety Board, on June 12, 2001, made the following safety recommendation to the FRA:

R-01-6

Facilitate actions necessary for development and implementation of positive train control systems that include collision avoidance, and require implementation of positive train control systems on main line tracks, establishing priority requirements for high-risk corridors such as those where commuter and intercity passenger railroads operate.

The CSXT Chicago line in this accident is the same line that was involved in the Bryan, Ohio, accident. Since the line carries intercity passenger traffic, it should be subject to the priority need identified in the recommendation. As of October 29, 2001, the Safety Board had received no response from the FRA to this recommendation.

The absence of a positive train control system is of particular concern where passenger trains operate because of the number of lives that can be put at risk in the event of human error. In the view of the Safety Board, the risk of operating without a fail-safe train control system may be exacerbated when passenger trains operate with a single crewmember in the operating compartment.

Passenger trains have operated with only one person in the locomotive cab along the Northeast Corridor between Washington, D.C., and Boston, Massachusetts, since the 1960s, and Amtrak continues lone-engineer operation along that route today. However, the safety of lone-engineer operation on the Northeast Corridor is enhanced by a fail-safe train control system, known as the advanced train control system,[31] that helps prevent collisions. But Amtrak routinely employs lone-engineer operation systemwide in locations, such as the Syracuse area, where no redundant train control system is in place.

Amtrak asserts that locomotive alerters help ensure that lone-engineer operation is safe. But alerters cannot prevent an engineer from misreading a signal, speeding, or

---

[30] National Transportation Safety Board, *Collision Involving Three Consolidated Rail Corporation Freight Trains Operating in Fog at Bryan, Ohio, January 17, 1999*, Railroad Accident Report RAR-01/01 (Washington, D.C.: NTSB, 2001).

[31] The advanced train control system (ATC) will intervene to slow or stop a train in response to a signal indication should an engineer fail to do so. However, it does not enforce curve or other non-signaled speed restrictions well, nor does it enforce positive stops at interlocking home signals. A new system, advanced civil speed enforcement system (ACSES) is currently being installed to overlay the ATC system and overcome the limitations of that system. ACSES is already in place on about 198 miles of track along the Northeast Corridor.

colliding with another train, as in this accident. Alerters can only help ensure the engineer is responsive to cues and is, to some degree, "alert"; they cannot ensure that an engineer will make no mistakes or intervene if the engineer does make a mistake. Alerters are therefore not a replacement for safety redundancies such as positive train control, or even automatic train stop, nor can they always substitute for another person in the cab who could question the actions of the engineer.

In the view of the Safety Board, lone-engineer operation in areas where no positive train control system is in place may result in additional risk in the event of human error. Transport Canada recognized this potential additional risk and has addressed lone-engineer operation by, for example, requiring additional training and supervision of engineers or by requiring proximity detection devices for those railroad lines wishing to pursue lone-engineer operation. Some of the requirements developed by Transport Canada to address any additional risk presented by lone-engineer operation may be appropriate for U.S. railroads. The Safety Board therefore believes the FRA should evaluate the applicability to U.S. operations of the safety requirements established by Transport Canada for lone-engineer operation on the Quebec North Shore & Labrador Railway, and implement any found to have interim utility for U.S. passenger trains that operate in areas now lacking a system of positive train control.

Milepost Locations for Emergency Response

There was some initial confusion concerning the exact location of the accident when the CSXT dispatcher reported the accident to the Onondaga Emergency Communications Center. The confusion occurred primarily because the location that was provided referred to a railroad milepost and also to a street location. But the street location was actually about a mile from the accident, and, while the milepost location was accurate, the Onondaga Emergency Communications Center did not have a way to associate a milepost location with a street location or landmark. The Safety Board therefore concludes that in the emergency response to this accident, some initial confusion about the accident location occurred because the emergency response agency maps did not identify railroad milepost locations.

After a postaccident meeting between Amtrak representatives and all the accident emergency response organizations that responded to the Syracuse accident, the Onondaga County 911 Communications Control Center began including mileposts locations on its maps. This measure may allow responders to locate train accident sites more quickly and reliably. The Safety Board endorses such proactive action and believes the inclusion of railroad mileposts on emergency response maps throughout the United States could help minimize response times to railroad accidents. Therefore, the Safety Board believes that the National Emergency Number Association, with the cooperation of the Association of American Railroads and the American Short Line and Regional Railroad Association, should facilitate the inclusion of railroad milepost markers on all emergency response maps across the country.

Equipment Securement

After the accident, Safety Board investigators examining Amtrak café car 48910 found that a convection oven had been displaced and had shifted several inches out of its locked position. The retaining bar that is meant to secure the oven in place was found unlocked. Fortunately, no one was injured as a result of the oven's movement, as they had been in previous accidents where appliances had been unsecured.

As a result of its investigation of a December 19, 1989, accident in which an Amtrak train struck a truck semitrailer combination in Stockton, California,[32] the Safety Board made the following safety recommendation to Amtrak:

R-90-48

Establish system wide rules to ensure that only properly secured appliances are used in revenue service and to establish procedures for enforcing those rules.

On June 21, 1991, Amtrak responded:

The chief mechanical officer issued procedures to all field mechanical officers, which detail the requirement to utilize food service appliances that are compatible with available restraints. Division mechanical superintendents will ensure that cars are properly equipped with restraints during 120-day maintenance. They will also enforce the daily maintenance of applied restraint systems when appliances are replaced. In addition…all microwave, coffee, and convection oven restraints will be installed by 10/1/91.

Based on this response, the Safety Board classified Safety Recommendation R-90-48 "Closed Acceptable Action" on August 21, 1991.

As noted, while a restraint bar was in place on the convection oven in café car 48910, it was unlocked and did not secure the equipment. Furthermore, when Safety Board investigators reviewed the passenger car maintenance requirements in the *Northeast Corridor 120-Day Preventive Maintenance Program Fiscal Year 2000* book, they found no requirement to ensure that appliances are secured and locked in place. Nor do daily or initial terminal inspections include securement check of appliances. The Safety Board therefore concludes that Amtrak procedures are inadequate for ensuring that food service appliances in passenger service are secured sufficiently to prevent their becoming a source of passenger or crew injury in the event of an accident.

The Safety Board therefore believes that Amtrak should modify its procedures, as appropriate, to ensure that all onboard appliances are properly secured.

---

[32] National Transportation Safety Board, *Collision Of Amtrak Passenger Train No. 708 on Atchison, Topeka And Santa Fe Railway With TAB Warehouse and Distribution Company Tractor Semi Trailer, Stockton, California, December 19, 1989*, Railroad/Highway Accident Report NTSB/RHR–90/01 (Washington, D.C.: NTSB, 1990).

Conclusions

Findings

1. Weather was not causal or contributory to the accident.

2. The wayside signal, before the accident, displayed a *restricting* aspect and functioned as designed.

3. Crewmember fatigue likely was not a factor in the accident, and drugs or alcohol did not cause or contribute to the accident.

4. Neither of the trains involved in this accident had a mechanical condition that caused or contributed to the collision.

5. The physical condition of the Amtrak engineer at the time of the accident did not significantly affect his ability to perceive and appropriately respond to the wayside signals or to properly control the train.

6. Had the Amtrak train been traveling at either the actual authorized *restricted speed* of 15 mph or less, or at the Amtrak engineer's perceived *medium approach* maximum speed of 30 mph, the Amtrak engineer would have been able to stop short of the freight train.

7. Had a fail-safe safety redundancy system such as positive train control been installed and operational throughout the accident area, the accident would probably not have occurred.

8. In the emergency response to this accident, some initial confusion about the accident location occurred because the emergency response agency maps did not identify railroad milepost locations.

9. Amtrak procedures are inadequate for ensuring that food service appliances in passenger service are secured sufficiently to prevent their becoming a source of passenger or crew injury in the event of an accident.

Probable Cause

The National Transportation Safety Board determines that the probable cause of the February 5, 2001, collision of Amtrak train 286 with the rear of CSXT freight train Q620 was the Amtrak engineer's inattention to the operation of his train, which led to his failure to recognize and comply with the speed limit imposed by the governing wayside signal, and the lack of any safety redundancy system capable of preventing a collision in the event of human failure.

Recommendations

As a result of its investigation of the February 5, 2001, collision of Amtrak train 286 with the rear of CSXT freight train Q620 at Syracuse, New York, the National Transportation Safety Board makes the following safety recommendations:

To the Federal Railroad Administration

Evaluate the applicability to U.S. operations of the safety requirements established by Transport Canada for lone-engineer operation on the Quebec North Shore & Labrador Railway, and implement any found to have interim utility for U.S. passenger trains that operate in areas now lacking a system of positive train control. (R-01-21)

To the National Emergency Number Association:

Facilitate the inclusion of railroad milepost markers on all emergency response maps across the country. (R-01-22)

To the Association of American Railroads:

To the American Short Line and Regional Railroad Association:

Work with the National Emergency Number Association to facilitate the inclusion of railroad milepost markers on all emergency response maps across the country. (R-01-23)

To the National Railroad Passenger Corporation:

Modify your procedures, as appropriate, to ensure that all onboard appliances are properly secured. (R-01-24)

BY THE NATIONAL TRANSPORTATION SAFETY BOARD

MARION C. BLAKEY
Chairman

JOHN A. HAMMERSCHMIDT
Member

CAROL J. CARMODY
Vice Chairman

JOHN J. GOGLIA
Member

GEORGE W. BLACK, JR.
Member

Adopted: November 27, 2001